Pictures from Brueghel

and other poems by

WILLIAM
CARLOS
WILLIAMS

Collected Poems 1950-1962

A NEW DIRECTIONS BOOK

Of the poems in this volume, the "Pictures from Brueghel" sequence first appeared in *The Hudson Review*. Others appeared originally in the following magazines, to which acknowledgment is here made: *The Atlantic Monthly, Art News Annual, Botteghe Oscure, Chicago Review, College Music Symposium* of the Moravian Music Foundation, Inc., *East & West, Epoch, Folio, Harper's, Hudson Review, Imagi, Kavita, The Kenyon Review, London Times Literary Supplement, Massachusetts Review, National Review, New England Galaxy, New Poems by American Poets, New Ventures, New World Writing, New York Times Book Review, The New Yorker, Origin, Pennsylvania Literary Review, Poetry, Poetry Australia, Quarterly Review of Literature, Saturday Review, 7 Arts, Transatlantic Review.*

Acknowledgment is also made to The Lockwood Memorial Library, University of Buffalo, and The Yale University Library for access to their collections of Williams manuscripts.

Library of Congress Catalog Card Number: 62-10410.
First published as ND Paperbook 118 (ISBN: 0-8112-0234-8) in 1962
Clothbound edition (ISBN: 0-8112-0434-0) 1967.

Manufactured in the United States of America.
Published in Canada by George J. McLeod, Ltd.

New Directions Books are published for James Laughlin
by New Directions Publishing Corporation,
80 Eighth Avenue, New York 10011.

TWELFTH PRINTING

Contents

Pictures from Brueghel

". . . the form of a man's rattle may be in
accordance with instructions received in the
dream by which he obtained his power."

Frances Densmore
The Study of Indian Music

Pictures from Brueghel

I SELF-PORTRAIT

In a red winter hat blue
eyes smiling
just the head and shoulders

crowded on the canvas
arms folded one
big ear the right showing

the face slightly tilted
a heavy wool coat
with broad buttons

gathered at the neck reveals
a bulbous nose
but the eyes red-rimmed

from over-use he must have
driven them hard
but the delicate wrists

show him to have been a
man unused to
manual labor unshaved his

blond beard half trimmed
no time for any-
thing but his painting

According to Brueghel
when Icarus fell
it was spring

a farmer was ploughing
his field
the whole pageantry

of the year was
awake tingling
near

the edge of the sea
concerned
with itself

sweating in the sun
that melted
the wings' wax

unsignificantly
off the coast
there was

a splash quite unnoticed
this was
Icarus drowning

III THE HUNTERS IN THE SNOW

The over-all picture is winter
icy mountains
in the background the return

from the hunt it is toward evening
from the left
sturdy hunters lead in

their pack the inn-sign
hanging from a
broken hinge is a stag a crucifix

between his antlers the cold
inn yard is
deserted but for a huge bonfire

that flares wind-driven tended by
women who cluster
about it to the right beyond

the hill is a pattern of skaters
Brueghel the painter
concerned with it all has chosen

a winter-struck bush for his
foreground to
complete the picture .   .

IV   THE ADORATION OF THE KINGS

From the Nativity
which I have already celebrated
the Babe in its Mother's arms

the Wise Men in their stolen
splendor
and Joseph and the soldiery

attendant
with their incredulous faces
make a scene copied we'll say

from the Italian masters
but with a difference
the mastery

of the painting
and the mind the resourceful mind
that governed the whole

the alert mind dissatisfied with
what it is asked to
and cannot do

accepted the story and painted
it in the brilliant
colors of the chronicler

the downcast eyes of the Virgin
as a work of art
for profound worship

V PEASANT WEDDING

Pour the wine bridegroom
where before you the
bride is enthroned her hair

loose at her temples a head
of ripe wheat is on
the wall beside her the

guests seated at long tables
the bagpipers are ready
there is a hound under

the table the bearded Mayor
is present women in their
starched headgear are

gabbing all but the bride
hands folded in her
lap is awkwardly silent simple

dishes are being served
clabber and what not
from a trestle made of an

unhinged barn door by two
helpers one in a red
coat a spoon in his hatband

VI HAYMAKING

The living quality of
the man's mind
stands out

and its covert assertions
for art, art, art!
painting

that the Renaissance
tried to absorb
but

it remained a wheat field
over which the
wind played

men with scythes tumbling
the wheat in
rows

the gleaners already busy
it was his own—
magpies

the patient horses no one
could take that
from him

VII   THE CORN HARVEST

Summer!
the painting is organized
about a young

reaper enjoying his
noonday rest
completely

relaxed
from his morning labors
sprawled

in fact sleeping
unbuttoned
on his back

the women
have brought him his lunch
perhaps

a spot of wine
they gather gossiping
under a tree

whose shade
carelessly
he does not share the

resting
center of
their workaday world

Disciplined by the artist
to go round
& round

in holiday gear
a riotously gay rabble of
peasants and their

ample-bottomed doxies
fills
the market square

featured by the women in
their starched
white headgear

they prance or go openly
toward the wood's
edges

round and around in
rough shoes and
farm breeches

mouths agape
Oya!
kicking up their heels

This horrible but superb painting
the parable of the blind
without a red

in the composition shows a group
of beggars leading
each other diagonally downward

across the canvas
from one side
to stumble finally into a bog

where the picture
and the composition ends back
of which no seeing man

is represented the unshaven
features of the des-
titute with their few

pitiful possessions a basin
to wash in a peasant
cottage is seen and a church spire

the faces are raised
as toward the light
there is no detail extraneous

to the composition one
follows the others stick in
hand triumphant to disaster

I

This is a schoolyard
crowded
with children

of all ages near a village
on a small stream
meandering by

where some boys
are swimming
bare-ass

or climbing a tree in leaf
everything
is motion

elder women are looking
after the small
fry

a play wedding a
christening
nearby one leans

hollering
into
an empty hogshead

Little girls
whirling their skirts about
until they stand out flat

tops pinwheels
to run in the wind with
or a toy in 3 tiers to spin

with a piece
of twine to make it go
blindman's-buff follow the

leader stilts
high and low tipcat jacks
bowls hanging by the knees

standing on your head
run the gauntlet
a dozen on their backs

feet together kicking
through which a boy must pass
roll the hoop or a

construction
made of bricks
some mason has abandoned

III

The desperate toys
of children
their

imagination equilibrium
and rocks
which are to be

found
everywhere
and games to drag

the other down
blindfold
to make use of

a swinging
weight
with which

at random
to bash in the
heads about

them
Brueghel saw it all
and with his grim

humor faithfully
recorded
it

Exercise

Maybe it's his wife
the car is an official car
belonging

to a petty police officer
I think
but her get-up

was far from official
for that time
of day

Song

beauty is a shell
from the sea
where she rules triumphant
till love has had its way with her

scallops and
lion's paws
sculptured to the
tune of retreating waves

undying accents
repeated till
the ear and the eye lie
down together in the same bed

The Woodthrush

fortunate man it is not too late
the woodthrush
flies into my garden

before the snow
he looks at me silent without
moving

his dappled breast reflecting
tragic winter
thoughts my love my own

The Polar Bear

his coat resembles the snow
deep snow
the male snow
which attacks and kills

silently as it falls muffling
the world
to sleep that
the interrupted quiet return

to lie down with us
its arms
about our necks
murderously a little while

16

The Loving Dexterity

The flower
        fallen
she saw it

        where
it lay
        a pink petal

intact
        deftly
placed it

        on
its stem
        again

The Chrysanthemum

how shall we tell
the bright petals
from the sun in the
sky concentrically

crowding the branch
save that it yields
in its modesty
to that splendor?

3 Stances

poised for the leap she
is not yet ready for
—save in her eyes

her bare toes
starting over the clipt
lawn where she may

not go emphasize summer
and the curl
of her blonde hair

the tentative smile
for the adult plans laid
to trap her

calves beginning to flex
wrists
set for the getaway

II: ERICA

the melody line is
everything
in this composition

when I first witnessed
your head
and held it

admiringly between
my fingers
I bowed

my approval
at the Scandinavian
name they'd

given you Erica after
your father's
forebears

the rest remains a
mystery
your snub nose spinning

on the bridge of it
points the way
inward

III: EMILY

your long legs
built
to carry high

the small head
your
grandfather

knows
if he knows
anything

gives
the dance as
your genius

the cleft in
your
chin's curl

permitting
may it
carry you far

Suzy

I

women your age have decided
wars and the beat
of poems your grandfather

is a poet and loves you
pay attention
to your lessons an inkling

of what beauty means to
a girl your age
may dawn soon upon you

II

life is a flower when it
opens you will
look trembling into it unsure

of what the traditional
mirror may reveal
between hope and despair while

a timorous old man
doubtfully half
turns away his foolish head

III

a bunch of violets clutched
in your idle
hand gives him a place

beside you which he cherishes
his back turned
from you casually appearing

not to look he yearns after
you protectively
hopelessly wanting nothing

Paul

I

when you shall arrive
as deep
as you will need go

to catch the blackfish
the hook
has been featly baited

by the art you have
and
you do catch them

II

with what thoroughness
you know
seize that glistening

body translated
to
that language you

will understand gut
clean
roast garnish and

serve to yourself who
better
eat and enjoy

however you
divide
and share

that blackfish heft
and shine
is your own

Fragment

as for him who
finds fault
may silliness

and sorrow
overtake him
when you wrote

you did not
know
the power of

your words

To a Woodpecker

December bird in the bare tree
your harsh cry sounds
reminding me

of death we celebrated by lamen-
tations crying out
in the old

days wails of anguish shrieking
wakes curses that the
gods

had been so niggardly sweet
nightingale of the
winter

woods hang out the snow as if
it were gay
curtains

Song

I'd rather read an account
of a hidden
Carolina swamp where

the white heron breeds
protected from
the hunters reached only across

half-sunken logs a place
difficult of access the females
building their nests

in the stifling heat the males
in their mating splendor
than to witness

her broad pelvis
making her awkward at the
getaway . . .

but I have forgot beauty
that is no more than a sop
when our time

is spent and infirmities
bring us to
eat out of the same bowl!

The Children

Once in a while
we'd find a patch
of yellow violets

not many
but blue big blue
ones in

the cemetery woods
we'd pick
bunches of them

there was a family
named Foltette
a big family

with lots of children's graves
so we'd take

bunches of violets
and place one
on each headstone

The Painting

Starting from black or
finishing
with it

her defeat stands
a delicate
lock

of blonde hair dictated
by the
Sorbonne

this was her last
clear
act

a portrait of a
child
to which

she was indifferent
beautifully
drawn

then she married and
moved to
another country

The Stone Crock

In my hand I hold
a postcard
addressed to me
    by a lady

Stoneware crock
salt-glazed
a dandelion embossed
    dark blue

She selected it
for me to
admire casually
    in passing

she was a Jewess
intimate of
a man I
    admired

We often met in
her studio
and talked
    of him

he loved the early
art of this
country
    blue stoneware

stamped on the
bulge of it
Albany reminding me
    of him

Now he is dead how
gentle he
was and
            persistent

He Has Beaten about the Bush Long Enough

What a team
Flossie, Mary, a chemistry prof
and I

make to confront
the
slowly hardening

brain
of an academician
The most

that can be said
for it
is

that it has the crystal-
line pattern
of

new ice on
a country
pool

Iris

a burst of iris so that
come down for
breakfast

we searched through the
rooms for
that

sweetest odor and at
first could not
find its

source then a blue as
of the sea
struck

startling us from among
those trumpeting
petals

Song

you are forever April
to me
the eternally unready

forsythia a blonde
straight-
legged girl

whom I myself
ignorant
as I was taught

to read the poems
my arms
about your neck

we clung together
peril-
ously

more than a young
girl
should know

a burst of frost
nipped
yellow flowers

in the spring
of
the year

The Dance

When the snow falls the flakes
spin upon the long axis
that concerns them most intimately
two and two to make a dance

the mind dances with itself,
taking you by the hand,
your lover follows
there are always two,

yourself and the other,
the point of your shoe setting the pace,
if you break away and run
the dance is over

Breathlessly you will take
another partner
better or worse who will keep
at your side, at your stops

whirls and glides until he too
leaves off
on his way down as if
there were another direction

gayer, more carefree
spinning face to face but always down
with each other secure
only in each other's arms

But only the dance is sure!
make it your own.
Who can tell
what is to come of it?

in the woods of your
own nature whatever
twig interposes, and bare twigs
have an actuality of their own

this flurry of the storm
that holds us,
plays with us and discards us
dancing, dancing as may be credible.

Jersey Lyric

view of winter trees
before
one tree

in the foreground
where
by fresh-fallen

snow
lie 6 woodchunks ready
for the fire

To the Ghost of Marjorie Kinnan Rawlings

To celebrate your brief life
as you lived it grimly
under attack as it happens
to any common soldier
black or white
surrounded by the heavy scent
of orange blossoms solitary
in your low-lying farm among the young trees

Wise and gentle-voiced
old colored women
attended you among the reeds
and polonia
with its blobs of purple
flowers your pup smelling of
skunk beside your grove-men
lovesick maids and
one friend of the same sex
who knew how to handle a boat in a swamp

Your quick trips to your
New York publisher
beating your brains out
over the composition
under the trees to the tune
of a bull got loose
gathering the fruit and
preparing new fields to be put under the plough

You lived nerves drawn
tense beside dogtooth violets
bougainvillaea swaying
rushes and yellow jasmine

that smells so sweet
young and desperate
as you were taking chances
sometimes that you should be
thrown from the saddle
and get your neck broke
as it must have happened and it did in the end

To Be Recited to Flossie on Her Birthday

Let him who may
among the continuing lines
seek out

that tortured constancy
affirms
where I persist

let me say
across cross purposes
that the flower bloomed

struggling to assert itself
simply under
the conflicting lights

you will believe me
a rose
to the end of time

Metric Figure

gotta hold your nose
with the appropriate gesture
smiling

back of
the garbage truck
as the complex

city passes
to the confession
or psychiatric couch or booth

The Intelligent Sheepman and the New Cars

I'd like to
pull
the back out

and use
one of them
to take

my "girls"
to
the fairs in

The Italian Garden

When she married years ago
her romantic ideas dominated
the builders

nightingale and hermit thrush
then the garden
fell into disuse.

Now her son has taken up her
old ideas formally
shut out

by high walls from the sheep run.
It is a scene from Comus
transported

to upper New York State. I remember
it already ruined
in

early May the trees crowded
with orioles chickadees
robins

brown-thrashers cardinals
in their scarlet
coats

vocal at dawn among pools
reft of their
lilies

and rarer plants flowers
given instead to
mallows

pampas-grass and cattails by
drought and winter
winds

where now hummingbirds touch
without touching.
Moss-covered

benches fallen apart among
sunken gardens
where

The Faerie Queene was read to
strains from
Campion

and the scent of wild strawberries
mingled with that
of eglantine

and verbena. Courtesy has revived
with visitors who
have

begun to stroll the paths
as in the quattrocentro
covertly.

Maybe it will drive them to
be more civil
love

more jocosely (a good word) as
we presume they did
in that famous

garden where Boccaccio and
his friends hid
themselves

from the plague and rude manners
in the woods
of that garden

as we would similarly today
to escape the plague
of

our cars which cannot
penetrate
hers.

Poem

The rose fades
and is renewed again
by its seed, naturally
but where

save in the poem
shall it go
to suffer no diminution
of its splendor

A Formal Design

This fleur-de-lis
at a fence rail
where a unicorn is

confined it is a tapestry
deftly woven
a milleflor

design the fleur-de-lis
with its yellow
petals edges

a fruiting tree formally
enough in
this climate

a pomegranate to which
a princely
collar round his

arching neck the beast
is lightly
tethered

Bird

Bird with outstretched
wings poised
inviolate unreaching

yet reaching
your image this November
planes

to a stop
miraculously fixed in my
arresting eyes

The Gossips

Blocking the sidewalk so
we had to go round
3 carefully coiffured
and perfumed old men
fresh from the barbers
a cartoon by Daumier
reflecting the times were
discussing with a foreign
accent one cupping his
ears not to miss a
syllable the news from
Russia on a view of
the reverse surface of
the moon

Exercise No. 2

The metal smokestack
of my neighbor's chimney
greets me among the new leaves

it is a small house
adjacent to my bigger one
I have come in 3 years

to know much of her
an old lady as I am an old man
we greet each other

across the hedge
my wife gives her flowers
we have never visited each other

The World Contracted to a Recognizable Image

at the small end of an illness
there was a picture
probably Japanese
which filled my eye

an idiotic picture
except it was all I recognized
the wall lived for me in that picture
I clung to it as to a fly

The Fruit

Waking
I was eating pears!
she said

I sat beside her on the bed
thinking
of Picasso

a portrait of
a sensitive young boy
gathered

into himself
Waking
I was eating pears!

she said
when separate jointly
we embraced

Short Poem

You slapped my face
oh but so gently
I smiled
at the caress

Poem

on getting a card
long delayed
from a poet whom I love
but

with whom I differ
touching
the modern poetic
technique

I was much moved
to hear
from him if
as yet he does not

concede the point
nor is he
indeed conscious of it
no matter

his style
has other outstanding
virtues
which delight me

To Flossie

who showed me
           a bunch of garden roses
she was keeping
           on ice

against an appointment
           with friends
for supper
           day after tomorrow

aren't they beautiful
           you can't
smell them
           because they're so cold

but aren't they
           in wax
paper for the
           moment beautiful

Portrait of a Woman at Her Bath

it is a satisfaction
a joy
to have one of those
in the house

when she takes a bath
she unclothes
herself she is no
Venus

I laugh at her
an Inca
shivering at the well
the sun is

glad of a fellow to
marvel at
the birds and the flowers
look in

Some Simple Measures in the American Idiom and the Variable Foot

I: EXERCISE IN TIMING

Oh
the sumac died
it's
the first time
I
noticed it

II: HISTOLOGY

There is
the
microscopic
anatomy

of
the whale
this is
reassuring

III: PERPETUUM MOBILE

To all the girls
of all ages
who walk up and down on

the streets of this town
silent or gabbing
putting

their feet down
one before the other
one two

one two they
pause sometimes before
a store window and

reform the line
from here
to China everywhere

back and
forth and back and forth
and back and forth

IV: THE BLUE JAY

It crouched
just before the take-off

caught
in the cinematograph—

in motion
of the mind wings

just set to spread a
flash a

blue curse
a memory of you

my friend
shrieked at me

—serving art
as usual

V: THE EXISTENTIALIST'S WIFE

I used to follow
the seasons
in this semi-northern

climate
and the warblers
that come

in May knew
the parula from
the myrtle

when I found it
dead on
the lawn there is

no season but
the one
for me now

VI: A SALAD FOR THE SOUL

My pleasant soul
we may not be destined to
survive our guts
let's celebrate

what we eject
sometimes

with greatest fervor
I hear it

also from the ladies' room
what ho!
the source
of all delicious salads

VII: CHLOE

The calves of
the young girls legs
when they are well made

knees
lithely built
in their summer clothes

show them
predisposed toward flight
or the dance

the magenta flower
of the
moth-mullen balanced

idly
tilting her weight
from one foot

to the other
shifting
to avoid looking at me

on my way to
mail a letter
smiling to a friend

VIII: THE COCKTAIL PARTY

A young woman
on whose belly I have never
slept though others

have
met today
at a cocktail party

not drunk
but by love
ignoring the others

we looked in
each other's eyes
eyes alert to

what we were saying
eyes blinded
breathless by that alone

IX: THE STOLEN PEONIES

What I got out of women
was difficult
to assess Flossie

not you
you lived with me
many years you remember

that year
we had the magnificent
stand of peonies

how happy we were
with them
but one night

they were stolen
we shared the
loss together thinking

of nothing else for
a whole day
nothing could have

brought us closer
we had been
married ten years

The High Bridge above the
Tagus River at Toledo

A young man, alone, on the high bridge over the Tagus which
    was too narrow to allow the sheep driven by the lean,
    enormous dogs whose hind legs worked slowly on cogs
to pass easily . . .
        (he didn't speak the language)

Pressed against the parapet either side by the crowding sheep,
    the relentless pressure of the dogs communicated
    itself to him also
above the waters in the gorge below.

They were hounds to him rather than sheep dogs because of
    their size and savage appearance, dog tired from the day's
    work.
The stiff jerking movement of the hind legs, the hanging
    heads at the shepherd's heels, slowly followed the excited
    and crowding sheep.

The whole flock, the shepherd and the dogs, were covered
    with dust as if they had been all day long on the road. The
    pace of the sheep, slow in the mass,
governed the man and the dogs. They were approaching the
    city at nightfall, the long journey completed.

In old age they walk in the old man's dreams and still walk
    in his dreams, peacefully continuing in his verse
    forever.

15 Years Later

on seeing my own play
Many Loves
on the stage for the first time

I recall
many a passage
of the original con-

versations with my
patients, especially the
women, myself

the interlocutor
laying myself bare for them
all there

in the play but who will
take the trouble
to evaluate

the serious aspects of
the case? One
of the actors by

dint of learning the lines
by heart
has come to me

his face aglow openmouthed
a light in his eyes
Nothing more

The Title

—as in Gauguin's *The Loss of Virginity*—
how inessential it is to the composition:

the nude body, unattended save by a watchful
hound, forepaw against the naked breast,

there she lies on her back in an open field,
limbs quietly assembled—yet how by its

very unrelatedness it enhances the impact
and emotional dignity of the whole . . .

Mounted as an Amazon

She rides her hips as
it were a horse
such women

tickle me a pat answer
to philosophy
or high heels would

put them on their
cans if fol-
lowed up most women

are more pliant
come of
a far different race

The Snow Begins

A rain of bombs, well placed,
is no less lovely
but this comes gently over all

all crevices are covered
the stalks of
fallen flowers vanish before

this benefice all the garden's
wounds are healed
white, white, white as death

fallen which dignifies it as
no violence ever can
gently and silently in the night.

Calypsos

I

Well God is
love
so love me

God
is love so
love me God

is
love so love
me well

II

Love the sun
comes
up in

the morning
and
in

the evening
zippy zappy
it goes

III

We watched
a red rooster
with

two hens
back
of the museum

at
St. Croix
flap his

wings
zippy zappy
and crow

An Exercise

Sick as I am
confused in the head
I mean I have

endured this April
so far
visiting friends

returning home
late at night
I saw

a huge Negro
a dirty collar
about his

enormous neck
appeared to be
choking

him
I did not know
whether or not

he saw me though
he was sitting
directly

before me how
shall we
escape this modern

age
and learn
to breathe again

Three Nahuatl Poems

One by one I proclaim your songs:
    I bind them on, gold crabs, as if they were anklets:
    like emeralds I gather them.
Clothe yourself in them: they are your riches.
    Bathe in feathers of the quetzal,
your treasury of birds' plumes, black and yellow,
the red feathers of the macaw
beat your drums about the world:
deck yourself out in them: they are your riches.

Where am I to go, whither?
    The road's there, the road to Two-Gods.
    Well, who checks men here,
here where all lack a body,
at the bottom of the sky?
Or, maybe, it is only on Earth
that we lose the body?
    Cleaned out, rid of it completely,
His House: there remains none on this earth!
Who is it that said:
Where find them? our friends no longer exist!

Will he return will Prince Cuautli ever return?
Will Ayocuan, the one who drove an arrow into the sky?
Shall these two yet gladden you?
    Events don't recur: we vanish once only.
Hence the cause of my weeping:
Prince Ayocuan, warrior chief
governed us harshly.
His pride waxed more, he grew haughty
here among men.
    But his time is finished . . .

he can no longer come to bow down before Father and
    Mother. . . .
This is the reason for my weeping:
He has fled to the place where all lack a body.

Sonnet in Search of an Author

Nude bodies like peeled logs
sometimes give off a sweetest
odor, man and woman

under the trees in full excess
matching the cushion of

aromatic pine-drift fallen
threaded with trailing woodbine
a sonnet might be made of it

Might be made of it! odor of excess
odor of pine needles, odor of
peeled logs, odor of no odor
other than trailing woodbine that

has no odor, odor of a nude woman
sometimes, odor of a man.

The Gift

As the wise men of old brought gifts
        guided by a star
                to the humble birthplace

of the god of love,
        the devils
                as an old print shows
retreated in confusion.

        What could a baby know
                of gold ornaments
or frankincense and myrrh,
        of priestly robes
                and devout genuflections?

But the imagination
        knows all stories
                before they are told
and knows the truth of this one
        past all defection

The rich gifts
        so unsuitable for a child
                though devoutly proffered,
stood for all that love can bring.

        The men were old
                how could they know
of a mother's needs
        or a child's
                appetite?

But as they kneeled
        the child was fed.

They saw it
and
gave praise!

A miracle
had taken place,
hard gold to love,
a mother's milk!
before
their wondering eyes.

The ass brayed
the cattle lowed.
It was their nature.

All men by their nature give praise.
It is all
they can do.

The very devils
by their flight give praise.
What is death,
beside this?

Nothing. The wise men
came with gifts
and bowed down
to worship
this perfection.

The Turtle

(For My Grandson)

Not because of his eyes,
            the eyes of a bird,
                        but because he is beaked,
birdlike, to do an injury,
            has the turtle attracted you.
                        He is your only pet.
When we are together
            you talk of nothing else
                        ascribing all sorts
of murderous motives
            to his least action.
                        You ask me
to write a poem,
            should I have poems to write,
                        about a turtle.

The turtle lives in the mud
            but is not mud-like,
                        you can tell it by his eyes
which are clear.
            When he shall escape
                        his present confinement
he will stride about the world
            destroying all
                        with his sharp beak.
Whatever opposes him
            in the streets of the city
                        shall go down.
Cars will be overturned.
            And upon his back
                        shall ride,

to his conquests,
           my Lord,
                      you!

You shall be master!
           In the beginning
                      there was a great tortoise
who supported the world.
           Upon him
                      all ultimately
rests.
           Without him
                      nothing will stand.
He is all wise
           and can outrun the hare.
                      In the night
his eyes carry him
           to unknown places.
                      He is your friend.

Sappho, Be Comforted

There is only one love
let it be a sparrow
to hold between the breasts
      greets us daily with its small cries

what does it matter?
I, we'll say, love a woman
but truth to tell
      I love myself more. Sappho loves

the music of her own
songs which men seldom
mean to her, a lovely girl
      of whom she is desperately fond:

This is myself though
my hateful mirror
shows every day my big nose.
      Men are indifferent to me, my sweet

but I would not trade
my skill in composition for
all, a second choice, you
      present for my passionate caresses.

To My Friend Ezra Pound

or he were a Jew or a
Welshman
I hope they do give you the Nobel Prize
it would serve you right
      —in perpetuity
with such a name

If I were a dog
I'd sit down on a cold pavement
in the rain
to wait for a friend (and so would you)
if it so pleased me
even if it were January or Zukofsky

Your English
is not specific enough
As a writer of poems
you show yourself to be inept not to say
usurious

Tapiola

He is no more dead than Finland herself is dead
under the blows of the mass-man who threatened
to destroy her until she felled her forests
about his head, ensnaring him. But, children, you
underestimated the power in your own song, *Finlandia!*
It holds you up but no more so than has he I celebrate
who had heard the icy wind in his ears and defied
it lovingly with a smile. The power of music,
of composition, the placing of sounds together,
edge against edge, Musorgski the half-mad Russian
had it and Dostoevski who knew the soul. In such
style whistled the winds grateful to be tamed,
we say, by a man. Whee-wow! You stayed up half
the night in your attic room under the eaves, composing
secretly, setting it down, period after period,
as the wind whistled. Lightning flashed! The roof
creaked about your ears threatening to give
way! But you had a composition to finish that could
not wait. The storm entered your mind where all
good things are secured, written down, for love's
sake and to defy the devil of emptiness. The
children are decked out in ribbons, bunting and
with flags in their hands to celebrate your birthday!
They parade to music! a joyous occasion. Sibelius
has been born and continues to live in all our
minds, all of us, forever. . . .

Poem

The plastic surgeon who has
concerned himself
with the repair of the mole

on my ear could not be
more pointedly
employed

let all men confess it
Gauguin or Van Gogh
were intimates

who fell out finally
and parted going
to the ends of the earth

to be apart, wild men
one of them cut
his ear off with a pair of shears

which made him none the less
a surpassing genius
this happened

yesterday forgive him
he was mad
and who among us has retained

his sanity or balance
in the course the
events have taken since those days

Heel & Toe to the End

Gagarin says, in ecstasy,
he could have
gone on forever

he floated
ate and sang
and when he emerged from that

one hundred eight minutes off
the surface of
the earth he was smiling

Then he returned
to take his place
among the rest of us

from all that division and
subtraction a measure
toe and heel

heel and toe he felt
as if he had
been dancing

The Rewaking

Sooner or later
we must come to the end
of striving

to re-establish
the image the image of
the rose

but not yet
you say extending the
time indefinitely

by
your love until a whole
spring

rekindle
the violet to the very
lady's-slipper

and so by
your love the very sun
itself is revived

The Desert Music and Other Poems

(1954)

To Bill and Paul

The Descent

The descent beckons
            as the ascent beckoned.
                        Memory is a kind
of accomplishment,
            a sort of renewal
                        even
an initiation, since the spaces it opens are new places
            inhabited by hordes
                        heretofore unrealized,
of new kinds—
            since their movements
                        are toward new objectives
(even though formerly they were abandoned).

No defeat is made up entirely of defeat—since
the world it opens is always a place
            formerly
                        unsuspected. A
world lost,
            a world unsuspected,
                        beckons to new places
and no whiteness (lost) is so white as the memory
of whiteness   .

With evening, love wakens
            though its shadows
                        which are alive by reason
of the sun shining—
            grow sleepy now and drop away
                        from desire   .

Love without shadows stirs now
          beginning to awaken
                    as night
advances.

The descent
          made up of despairs
                    and without accomplishment
realizes a new awakening:
                    which is a reversal
of despair.
          For what we cannot accomplish, what
is denied to love,
          what we have lost in the anticipation—
                    a descent follows,
endless and indestructible   .

To Daphne and Virginia

The smell of the heat is boxwood
        when rousing us
                a movement of the air
stirs our thoughts
        that had no life in them
                to a life, a life in which
two women agonize:
        to live and to breathe is no less.
                Two young women.
The box odor
        is the odor of that of which
                partaking separately,
each to herself
        I partake also
              .   .   separately.

Be patient that I address you in a poem,
        there is no other
                fit medium.
The mind
        lives there. It is uncertain,
                can trick us and leave us
agonized. But for resources
        what can equal it?
                There is nothing. We
should be lost
        without its wings to
                fly off upon.

The mind is the cause of our distresses
        but of it we can build anew.
                Oh something more than

it flies off to:
a woman's world,
of crossed sticks, stopping
thought. A new world
is only a new mind.
And the mind and the poem
are all apiece.
Two young women
to be snared,
odor of box,
to bind and hold them
for the mind's labors.

All women are fated similarly
facing men
and there is always
another, such as I,
who loves them,
loves all women, but
finds himself, touching them,
like other men,
often confused.

I have two sons,
the husbands of these women,
who live also
in a world of love,
apart.
Shall this odor of box in
the heat
not also touch them
fronting a world of women
from which they are
debarred
by the very scents which draw them on
against easy access?

In our family we stammer unless,
half mad,
we come to speech at last

And I am not
a young man.
My love encumbers me.
It is a love
less than
a young man's love but,
like this box odor
more penetrant, infinitely
more penetrant,
in that sense not to be resisted.

There is, in the hard
give and take
of a man's life with
a woman
a thing which is not the stress itself
but beyond
and above
that,
something that wants to rise
and shake itself
free. We are not chickadees
on a bare limb
with a worm in the mouth.
The worm is in our brains
and concerns them
and not food for our
offspring, wants to disrupt
our thought
and throw it
to the newspapers
or anywhere.

                    There is, in short,
a counter stress,
                    born of the sexual shock,
                              which survives it
consonant with the moon,
                    to keep its own mind.
                              There is, of course,
more.
          Women
                              are not alone
in that. At least
                    while this healing odor is abroad
                              one can write a poem.

Staying here in the country
                    on an old farm
                              we eat our breakfasts
on a balcony under an elm.
                    The shrubs below us
                              are neglected. And
there, penned in,
                    or he would eat the garden,
                              lives a pet goose who
tilts his head
                    sidewise
                              and looks up at us,
a very quiet old fellow
                    who writes no poems.
                              Fine mornings we sit there
while birds
          come and go.
                    A pair of robins
is building a nest   .
                    for the second time
                              this season. Men

against their reason
           speak of love, sometimes,
                      when they are old. It is
all they can do   .
           or watch a heavy goose
                    who waddles, slopping
                    noisily in the mud of
                    his pool.

The Orchestra

The precise counterpart
        of a cacophony of bird calls
                lifting the sun almighty
into his sphere: wood-winds
        clarinet and violins
                sound a prolonged A!
Ah! the sun, the sun! is about to rise
        and shed his beams
                as he has always done
upon us all,
        drudges and those
                who live at ease,
women and men,
        upon the old,
                upon children and the sick
who are about to die and are indeed
        dead in their beds,
                to whom his light
is forever lost. The cello
        raises his bass note
                manfully in the treble din:
Ah, ah and ah!
        together, unattuned
                seeking a common tone.
Love is that common tone
        shall raise his fiery head
                and sound his note.

The purpose of an orchestra
        is to organize those sounds
                and hold them
to an assembled order   .
        in spite of the

"wrong note." Well, shall we
think or listen? Is there a sound addressed
not wholly to the ear?
We half close
our eyes. We do not
hear it through our eyes.
It is not
a flute note either, it is the relation
of a flute note
to a drum. I am wide
awake. The mind
is listening. The ear
is alerted. But the ear
in a half-reluctant mood
stretches
.   .   and yawns.

And so the banked violins
in three tiers
enliven the scene,
pizzicato. For a short
memory or to
make the listener listen
the theme is repeated
stressing a variant:
it is a principle of music
to repeat the theme. Repeat
and repeat again,
as the pace mounts. The
theme is difficult   .
but no more difficult
than the facts to be
resolved. Repeat
and repeat the theme
and all it develops to be

until thought is dissolved
            in tears.
                        Our dreams
have been assaulted
            by a memory that will not
                        sleep. The
French horns
            interpose
                        .   .   their voices:
I love you. My heart
            is innocent. And this
                        the first day of the world!

Say to them:
"Man has survived hitherto because he was too **ignorant**
to know how to realize his wishes. Now that he **can realize**
them, he must either change them or perish."

Now is the time   .
            in spite of the "wrong note"
                        I love you. My heart is
innocent.
            And this the first
                        (and last) day of the world

The birds twitter now anew
            but a design
                        surmounts their twittering.
It is a design of a man
            that makes them twitter.
                        It is a design.

For Eleanor and Bill Monahan

Mother of God! Our Lady!
            the heart
                        is an unruly Master:
Forgive us our sins
            as we
                        forgive
those who have sinned against
            us.
                        We submit ourselves
to Your rule
            as the flowers in May
                        submit themselves to
                        Your Holy rule—against
that impossible springtime
            when men
                        shall be the flowers
spread at your feet.

As far as spring is
            from winter
                        so are we
from you now. We have not come
            easily
                        to your environs
but painfully
            across sands
                        that have scored our
feet. That which we have suffered
            was for us
                        to suffer. Now,
in the winter of the year,
            the birds who know how
                        to escape suffering

by flight
are gone. Man alone
is that creature who
cannot escape suffering
by flight   .

I do not come to you
save that I confess
to being
half man and half
woman. I have seen the ivy
cling
to a piece of crumbled
wall so that
you cannot tell
by which either
stands: this is to say
if she to whom I cling
is loosened both
of us go down.

Mother of God
I have seen you stoop
to a merest flower
and raise it
and press it to your cheek.
I could have called out
joyfully
but you were too far off.
You are a woman and
it was
a woman's gesture.

You have no lovers now
in the bare skies
to bring you flowers,

to whisper to you
          under a hedge
                    howbeit
you are young
          and fit to be loved.
                    I declare it boldly
with my heart
          in my teeth
                    and my knees knocking
together. Yet I declare
          it, and by God's word
                    it is no lie. Make us
humble and obedient to His rule.

There are men
          who as they live
                    fling caution to the
wind and women praise them
          and love them for it.
                    Cruel as the claws of
a cat   .   .

The moon which
          they have vulgarized recently
                    is still
your planet
          as it was Dian's before
                    you. What
do they think they will attain
          by their ships
                    that death has not
already given
          them? Their ships
                    should be directed
inward upon   .   But I
          am an old man. I
                    have had enough.

The female principle of the world
             is my appeal
                        in the extremity
to which I have come.
             O clemens! O pia! O dolcis!
                        Maria!

To a Dog Injured in the Street

It is myself,
             not the poor beast lying there
                        yelping with pain
that brings me to myself with a start—
             as at the explosion
                        of a bomb, a bomb that has laid
all the world waste.
             I can do nothing
                        but sing about it
and so I am assuaged
             from my pain.

A drowsy numbness drowns my sense
             as if of hemlock
                        I had drunk. I think
of the poetry
             of René Char
                        and all he must have seen
and suffered
             that has brought him
                        to speak only of

sedgy rivers,
      of daffodils and tulips
           whose roots they water,
even to the free-flowing river
      that laves the rootlets
           of those sweet-scented flowers
that people the
      milky
         way   .

I remember Norma
      our English setter of my childhood
           her silky ears
and expressive eyes.
      She had a litter
           of pups one night
in our pantry and I kicked
      one of them
           thinking, in my alarm,
that they
      were biting her breasts
           to destroy her.

I remember also
      a dead rabbit
           lying harmlessly
on the outspread palm
      of a hunter's hand.
           As I stood by
watching
      he took a hunting knife
           and with a laugh
thrust it
      up into the animal's private parts.
           I almost fainted.

Why should I think of that now?
            The cries of a dying dog
                        are to be blotted out
as best I can.
            René Char
                        you are a poet who believes
in the power of beauty
            to right all wrongs.
                        I believe it also.
With invention and courage
            we shall surpass
                        the pitiful dumb beasts,
let all men believe it,
            as you have taught me also
                        to believe it.

The Yellow Flower

What shall I say, because talk I must?
            That I have found a cure
                        for the sick?
I have found no cure
            for the sick   .
                        but this crooked flower
which only to look upon
            all men
                        are cured. This
is that flower
            for which all men
                        sing secretly their hymns
of praise. This
            is that sacred
                        flower!

Can this be so?
            A flower so crooked
                        and obscure? It is
a mustard flower
            and not a mustard flower,
                        a single spray
topping the deformed stem
            of fleshy leaves
                        in this freezing weather
under glass.

An ungainly flower and
            an unnatural one,
                        in this climate; what
can be the reason
            that it has picked me out
                        to hold me, openmouthed,

rooted before this window
            in the cold,
                        my will
drained from me
            so that I have only eyes
                        for these yellow,
twisted petals   .   ?

That the sight,
            though strange to me,
                        must be a common one,
is clear: there are such flowers
            with such leaves
                        native to some climate
which they can call
            their own.

But why the torture
            and the escape through
                        the flower? It is
as if Michelangelo
            had conceived the subject
                        of his *Slaves* from this
—or might have done so.
            And did he not make
                        the marble bloom? I
am sad
            as he was sad
                        in his heroic mood.
But also
            I have eyes
                        that are made to see and if
they see ruin for myself
            and all that I hold
                        dear, they see

also
                through the eyes
                        and through the lips
and tongue the power
        to free myself
                and speak of it, as
Michelangelo through his hands
        had the same, if greater,
                power.

Which leaves, to account for,
        the tortured bodies
                of
the slaves themselves
        and
                the tortured body of my flower
which is not a mustard flower at all
        but some unrecognized
                and unearthly flower
for me to naturalize
        and acclimate
                and choose it for my own.

The Host

According to their need,
        this tall Negro evangelist
                (at a table separate from the
                rest of his party);
these two young Irish nuns
        (to be described subsequently);
                and this white-haired Anglican
have come witlessly
        to partake of the host
                laid for them (and for me)
by the tired waitresses.

It is all
        (since eat we must)
                made sacred by our common need.
The evangelist's assistants
        are most open in their praise
                though covert
as would be seemly
        in such a public
                place. The nuns
are all black, a side view.
        The cleric,
                his head bowed to reveal
his unruly poll
        dines alone.

My eyes are restless.
        The evangelists eat well,
                fried oysters and what not
at this railway restaurant. The Sisters
        are soon satisfied. One
                on leaving,

looking straight before her under steadfast brows,
            reveals
                        blue eyes. I myself
have brown eyes
            and a milder mouth.

There is nothing to eat,
            seek it where you will,
                        but of the body of the Lord.
The blessed plants
            and the sea, yield it
                        to the imagination
intact. And by that force
            it becomes real,
                        bitterly
to the poor animals
            who suffer and die
                        that we may live.

The well-fed evangels,
            the narrow-lipped and bright-eyed nuns,
                        the tall,
white-haired Anglican,
            proclaim it by their appetites
                        as do I also,
chomping with my worn-out teeth:
            the Lord is my shepherd
                        I shall not want.

No matter how well they are fed,
            how daintily
                        they put the food to their lips,
it is all
            according to the imagination!
Only the imagination
            is real! They have imagined it,

                    therefore it is so:
of the evangels,
                with the long legs characteristic of the race—
                    only the docile women
of the party smiled at me
                when, with my eyes
                    I accosted them.
The nuns—but after all
                I saw only a face, a young face
                    cut off at the brows.
It was a simple story.
                The cleric, plainly
                    from a good school,
interested me more,
                a man with whom I might
                    carry on a conversation.

No one was there
                save only for
                    the food. Which I alone,
being a poet,
                could have given them.
                    But I
had only my eyes
                with which to speak.

Deep Religious Faith

Past death
          past rainy days
                    or the distraction
of lady's-smocks all silver-white;
          beyond the remote borders
                    of poetry itself
if it does not drive us,
          it is vain.
                    Yet it is
that which made El Greco
          paint his green and distorted saints
                    and live
lean.
          It is what in life drives us
                    to praise music
and the old
          or sit by a friend
                    in his last hours.

All that which makes the pear ripen
          or the poet's line
                    come true!
Invention is the heart of it.

Without the quirks
          and oddnesses of invention
                    the paralytic is confirmed
in his paralysis,
          it is from a northern
                    and half-savage country
where the religion
          is hate.

There
the citizens are imprisoned.
            The rose
                        may not be worshipped
or the poet look to it
            for benefit.

In the night a
            storm of gale proportions came
            up.
                        No one was there to envisage
a field of daisies!
            There were bellowings
                        and roarings
from a child's book
            of fairy tales,
                        the rumble
of a distant bombing
            —or of a bee!
                        Shame on our poets,
they have caught the prevalent fever:
            impressed
                        by the "laboratory,"
they have forgot
            the flower!
                        which goes beyond all
laboratories!
            They have quit the job
                        of invention. The
imagination has fallen asleep
            in a poppy-cup.

The Mental Hospital Garden

It is far to Assisi,
            but not too far:
                        Over this garden,
brooding over this garden,
            there is a kindly spirit,
                        brother to the poor
and who is poorer than he
            who is in love
                        when birds are nesting
in the spring of the year?
            They came
                        to eat from his hand
who had nothing,
            and yet
                        from his plenty
he fed them all.
            All mankind
                        grew to be his debtors,
a simple story.
            Love is in season.

At such a time,
            hyacinth time
                        in
the hospital garden,
            the time
                        of the coral-flowered
and early salmon-pink
            clusters, it is
                        the time also of
abandoned birds' nests
            before
                        the sparrows start
                        to tear them apart

against the advent of that bounty
                from which
                        they will build anew.

All about them
                on the lawns
                        the young couples
embrace   .
                as in a tale
                        by Boccaccio.
They are careless
                under license of the disease
                        which has restricted them
to these grounds.
                St. Francis forgive them
                        and all lovers
whoever they may be.
                They have seen
                        a great light, it
springs from their own bawdy foreheads.
                The light
                        is sequestered there
by these enclosing walls.
                They are divided
                        from their fellows.
It is a bounty
                from a last year's bird's nest.
                        St. Francis,
who befriended the wild birds,
                by their aid,
                        those who
have nothing
                and live
                        by the Holy light of love
that rules,
                blocking despair,
                        over this garden.

Time passes.
                    The pace has slackened
                                        But with the falling off
of the pace
            the scene has altered.
                                    The lovers raise their heads,
at that which has come over them.
                    It is summer now.
                                        The broad sun
shines!
            Blinded by the light
                                    they walk bewildered,
seeking
            between the leaves
                                for a vantage
from which to view
                    the advancing season.
                                        They are incredulous
of their own cure
                    and half minded
                                        to escape
into the dark again.
                    The scene
                                indeed has changed.
By St. Francis
                the whole scene
                                    has changed.
They glimpse
                a surrounding sky
                                    and the whole countryside.
Filled with terror
                    they seek
                                a familiar flower
at which to warm themselves,
                    but the whole field
                                        accosts them.
They hide their eyes

ashamed
before that bounty,
peering through their fingers
timidly.
The saint is watching,
his eyes filled with pity.

The year is still young
but not so young
as they
who face the fears
with which
they are confronted.
Reawakened
after love's first folly
they resemble children
roused from a long sleep.
Summer is here,
right enough.
The saint
has tactfully withdrawn.
One
emboldened,
parting the leaves before her,
stands in the full sunlight,
alone
shading her eyes
as her heart
beats wildly
and her mind
drinks up
the full meaning
of it
all!

The Artist

Mr. T.
            bareheaded
                        in a soiled undershirt
his hair standing out
            on all sides
                        stood on his toes
heels together
            arms gracefully
                        for the moment
curled above his head.
            Then he whirled about
                        bounded
into the air
            and with an *entrechat*
                        perfectly achieved
completed the figure.
            My mother
                        taken by surprise
where she sat
            in her invalid's chair
                        was left speechless.
Bravo! she cried at last
            and clapped her hands.
                        The man's wife
came from the kitchen:
            What goes on here? she said.
                        But the show was over.

Theocritus: Idyl I

A Version from the Greek

THYRSIS

The whisper of the wind in
        that pine tree,
                goatherd,
is sweet as the murmur of live water;
        likewise
                your flute notes. After Pan
you shall bear away second prize.
        And if he
                take the goat
with the horns,
        the she-goat
                is yours: but if
he choose the she-goat,
        the kid will fall
                to your lot.
And the flesh of the kid
        is dainty
                before they begin milking them.

GOATHERD

Your song is sweeter,
        shepherd,
                than the music
of the water as it plashes
        from the high face
                of yonder rock!
If the Muses

                    choose the young ewe
                            you shall receive
a stall-fed lamb
            as your reward,
                    but if
they prefer the lamb
        you
                    shall have the ewe for
                    second prize.

THYRSIS

Will you not, goatherd,
            in the Nymph's name
                    take your place on this
                    sloping knoll
among the tamarisks
            and pipe for me
                    while I tend my sheep.

GOATHERD

No, shepherd,
        nothing doing;
                it's not for us
to be heard during the noon hush.
        We dread Pan,
                who for a fact
is stretched out somewhere,
        dog tired from the chase;
                his mood is bitter,
anger ready at his nostrils.
        But, Thyrsis,
                since you are good at

singing of *The Afflictions of Daphnis*,
                and have most deeply
                                meditated the pastoral mode,
come here,
                let us sit down,
                                under this elm
facing Priapus and the fountain fairies,
                here where the shepherds come
                                to try themselves out
by the oak trees.
                Ah! may you sing
                                as you sang that day
facing Chromis out of Libya,
                I will let you milk, yes,
                                three times over,
a goat that is the mother of twins
                and even when
                                she has sucked her kids
her milk fills
                two pails. I will give besides,
                                new made, a two-eared bowl
of ivy-wood,
                rubbed with beeswax
                                that smacks still
of the knife of the carver.
                Round its upper edges
                                winds the ivy, ivy
flecked with yellow flowers
                and about it
                                is twisted
a tendril joyful with the saffron fruit.
                Within,
                                is limned a girl,
as fair a thing as the gods have made,
                dressed in a sweeping
                                gown.

Her hair
        is confined by a snood.
             Beside her
two fair-haired youths
        with alternate speech
           are contending
but her heart is
        untouched.
           Now,
she glances at one,
        smiling,
           and now, lightly
she flings the other a thought,
        while their eyes,
           by reason of love's
long vigils, are heavy
        but their labors
           all in vain.
In addition
        there is fashioned there
           an ancient fisherman
and a rock,
        a rugged rock,
           on which
with might and main
        the old man poises a great net
           for the cast
as one who puts his whole heart into it.
        One would say
           that he was fishing
with the full strength of his limbs
        so big do his muscles stand out
           about the neck.
Gray-haired though he be,
        he has the strength
           of a young man.

Now, separated
                from the sea-broken old man
                        by a narrow interval
is a vineyard,
            heavy
                    with fire-red clusters,
and on a rude wall
            sits a small boy
                    guarding them.
Round him
            two she-foxes are skulking.
                        One
goes the length of the vine-rows
            to eat the grapes
                    while the other
brings all her cunning to bear,
            by what has been set down,
                        vowing
she will never quit the lad
            until
                    she leaves him bare
and breakfastless.
            But the boy
                    is plaiting a pretty
cage of locust stalks and asphodel,
            fitting in the reeds
                    and cares less for his scrip
and the vines
            than he takes delight
                    in his plaiting.
All about the cup
            is draped the mild acanthus
                    a miracle of varied work,
a thing for you to marvel at.
            I paid
                    a Caledonian ferryman

a goat and a great white
            cream-cheese
                        for the bowl.
It is still virgin to me,
            its lip has never touched mine.
                        To gain my desire,
I would gladly
            give this cup
                        if you, my friend,
will sing for me
            that delightful song.
                        I hold nothing back.
Begin, my friend,
            for you cannot,
                        you may be sure,
take your song,
            which drives all things out of mind,
                        with you to the other world.

The Desert Music

—the dance begins: to end about a form
propped motionless—on the bridge
between Juárez and El Paso—unrecognizable
in the semi-dark

Wait!

The others waited while you inspected it,
on the very walk itself

Is it alive?

—neither a head,
legs nor arms!

It isn't a sack of rags someone
has abandoned here   torpid against
the flange of the supporting girder   ?

an inhuman shapelessness,
knees hugged tight up into the belly

Egg-shaped!

What a place to sleep!
on the International Boundary.   Where else,
interjurisdictional, not to be disturbed?

How shall we get said what must be said?

Only the poem.

Only the counted poem, to an exact measure:
to imitate, not to copy nature, not
to copy nature

NOT, prostrate, to copy nature
                              but a dance! to dance
two and two with him—
                    sequestered there asleep,
                              right end up!

      A music
supersedes his composure, hallooing to us
across a great distance   .   .

                              wakens the dance
who blows upon his benumbed fingers!

                              Only the poem
only the made poem, to get said what must
be said, not to copy nature, sticks
in our throats   .

The law?   The law gives us nothing
but a corpse, wrapped in a dirty mantle.
The law is based on murder and confinement,
long delayed,
but this, following the insensate music,
is based on the dance:

                    an agony of self-realization
bound into a whole
by that which surrounds us   .

                              I cannot escape

I cannot vomit it up

109

Only the poem!

Only the made poem, the verb calls it
                                    into being.

                    —it looks too small for a man.
A woman.   Or a very shriveled old man.
Maybe dead.   They probably inspect the place
and will cart it away later   .

                    Heave it into the river.
A good thing.

Leaving California to return east, the fertile desert,
                    (were it to get water)
surrounded us, a music of survival, subdued, distant, half
                    heard; we were engulfed
by it as in the early evening, seeing the wind lift
                    and drive the sand, we
passed Yuma. All night long, heading for El Paso to
                    meet our friend,
we slept fitfully.   Thinking of Paris, I waked to the tick
                    of the rails.   The
jagged desert   .

                    —to tell
what subsequently I saw and what heard

                    —to place myself (in
my nature) beside nature

                    —to imitate
nature (for to copy nature would be a
      shameful thing)

                    I lay myself down:

The Old Market's a good place to begin:
Let's cut through here—

                                 tequila's only
a nickel a slug in these side streets.
Keep out though.   Oh, it's all right at
this time of day but I saw H. terribly
beaten up in one of those joints.   He
asked for it.   I thought he was going to
be killed.   I do
my drinking on the main drag   .

                          That's the bull ring
Oh, said Floss, after she got used to the
change of light   .
                        What color!   Isn't it
wonderful!

       —paper flowers (*para los santos*)
baked red-clay utensils, daubed
with blue, silverware,
dried peppers, onions, print goods, children's
clothing   . the place deserted all but
for a few Indians squatted in the
booths, unnoticing (don't you think it)
as though they slept there   .

       There's a second tier.   Do you
want to go up?

       What makes Texans so tall?
We saw a woman this morning in a mink cape
six feet if she was an inch.   What a woman!

Probably a Broadway figure.

—tell you what else we saw: about a million
sparrows screaming their heads off

in the trees of that small park where
the buses stop, sanctuary,
I suppose,
from the wind driving the sand in that way
about the city   .

                              Texas rain they call it

—and those two alligators in the fountain   .

There were four

                    I saw only two

                              They were looking
right at you all the time   .

Penny please!   Give me penny please, mister.

                              Don't give them anything.

                                        .   instinctively
one has already drawn one's naked
wrist away from those obscene fingers
as in the mind a vague apprehension speaks
and the music rouses   .

                              Let's get in here.
                    a music!   cut off as
the bar door closes behind us.

                    We've got
another half hour.

                    —returned to the street,
the pressure moves from booth to booth along

the curb.   Opposite, no less insistent
the better stores are wide open.   Come in
and look around.   You don't have to buy: hats,
riding boots, blankets   .

              Look at the way,
slung from her neck with a shawl, that young
Indian woman carries her baby!

                  —a stream of Spanish,
as she brushes by, intense, wide-
eyed in eager talk with her boy husband

—three half-grown girls, one of them eating a
pomegranate.   Laughing.

                  and the serious tourist,
man and wife, middle-aged, middle-western,
their arms loaded with loot, whispering
together—still looking for bargains   .

                  and the aniline
red and green candy at the little booth
tended by the old Indian woman.
        Do you suppose anyone actually
buys—and eats the stuff?

My feet are beginning to ache me.

              We still got a few minutes.
Let's try here.   They had the mayor
up last month for taking $3000 a week from
the whorehouses of the city.   Not much left
for the girls.   There's a show on.

              Only a few tables
occupied.   A conventional orchestra—this

place livens up later—playing the usual local
jing-a-jing—a boy and girl team, she
                              confidential with someone
off stage.   Laughing: just finishing the act.

So we drink until the next turn—a strip tease.

Do you mean it?   Wow!   Look at her.

                              You'd have to be
pretty drunk to get any kick out of that.
She's no Mexican.   Some worn-out trouper from
the States.   Look at those breasts

       There is a fascination
       seeing her shake
       the beaded sequins from
       a string about her hips

       She gyrates but it's
       not what you think,
       one does not laugh
       to watch her belly.

       One is moved but not
       at the dull show.   The
       guitarist yawns.   She
       cannot even sing.   She

       has about her painted
       hardihood a screen
       of pretty doves which
       flutter their wings.

       Her cold eyes perfunc-
       torily moan but do not

smile.   Yet they bill
and coo by grace of
a certain candor.   She

is heavy on her feet.
That's good.   She
bends forward leaning
on the table of the
balding man sitting
upright, alone, so that
everything hangs for-
ward.
      What the hell
are you grinning
to yourself about?   Not
at *her?*
      The music!
I like her.   She fits

the music   .

Why don't these Indians get over this nauseating
prattle about their souls and their loves and sing
us something else for a change?

This place is rank
with it.   She
at least knows she's
part of another tune,
knows her customers,
has the same
opinion of them as I
have.   That gives her
one up   .   one up
following the lying
music   .

There is another music. The bright-colored candy
of her nakedness lifts her unexpectedly
to partake of its tune   .

                        Andromeda of those rocks,
the virgin of her mind   .   those unearthly
greens and reds
                        in her mockery of virtue
she becomes unaccountably virtuous   .
                        though she in no
way pretends it   .

Let's get out of this.

                        In the street it hit
me in the face as we started to walk again.   Or
am I merely playing the poet?   Do I merely invent
it out of whole cloth?   I thought   .

            What in the form of an old whore in
            a cheap Mexican joint in Juárez, her bare
            can waggling crazily can be
            so refreshing to me, raise to my ear
            so sweet a tune, built of such slime?

            Here we are. They'll be along any minute.
            The bar is at the right of the entrance,
            a few tables opposite which you have to pass
            to get to the dining room, beyond.

            A foursome, two oversize Americans, no
            longer young, got up as cowboys,
            hats and all, are drunk and carrying on
            with their gals, drunk also,

            especially one inciting her man, the
            biggest, *Yip ee*! to dance in

116

the narrow space, oblivious to everything
—she is insatiable and he is trying

stumblingly to keep up with her.
Give it the gun, pardner! *Yip ee*! We
pushed by them to our table, seven
of us.   Seated about the room

were quiet family groups, some with
children, eating.   Rather a better
class than you notice
on the streets.   So here we are.   You

can see through into the kitchen
where one of the cooks, his shirt sleeves
rolled up, an apron over
the well-pressed pants of a street

suit, black hair neatly parted,
a tall
good-looking man, is working
absorbed, before a chopping block

Old fashioneds all around?

                    So this is William
Carlos Williams, the poet   .

          Floss and I had half consumed
our quartered hearts of lettuce before
we noticed the others hadn't touched theirs   .
You seem quite normal.   Can you tell me?   Why
does one want to write a poem?

     Because it's there to be written.

Oh.   A matter of inspiration then?

                                        Of necessity.

Oh.   But what sets it off?

                    I am that he whose brains
                    are scattered
                                aimlessly

                                        —and so,
the hour done, the quail eaten, we were on
our way back to El Paso.

                                Good night.   Good
night and thank you . No. Thank you. We're
going to walk   .

—and so, on the naked wrist, we feel again
those insistent fingers   .

                                Penny please, mister.
Penny please.   Give me penny.

                                Here! now go away.

—but the music, the music has reawakened
as we leave the busier parts of the street
and come again to the bridge in the semi-dark,
pay our fee and begin again to cross   .
seeing the lights along the mountain back of El
Paso and pause to watch the boys calling out
to us to throw more coins to them standing
in the shallow water   .   so that's
where the incentive lay, with the annoyance
of those surprising fingers.

                                So you're a poet?
a good thing to be got rid of—half drunk,

a free dinner under your belt, even though you
get typhoid—and to have met people you
can at least talk to   .

                  relief from that changeless, endless
inescapable and insistent music   .

             What else, Latins, do you yourselves
seek but relief!
with the expressionless ding dong you dish up
to us of your souls and your loves, which
we swallow. Spaniards! (though these are mostly
Indians who chase the white bastards
through the streets on their Independence Day
and try to kill them)   .

                              What's that?
Oh, come on.

             But what's THAT?

                          the music! the
music! as when Casals struck
and held a deep cello tone
and I am speechless   .

                              There it sat
in the projecting angle of the bridge flange
as I stood aghast and looked at it—
in the half-light: shapeless or rather returned
to its original shape, armless, legless,
headless, packed like the pit of a fruit into
that obscure corner—or
a fish to swim against the stream—or
a child in the womb prepared to imitate life,

119

warding its life against
a birth of awful promise.   The music
guards it, a mucus, a film that surrounds it,
a benumbing ink that stains the
sea of our minds—to hold us off—shed
of a shape close as it can get to no shape,
a music! a protecting music   .

                                        I *am* a poet! I
am.   I am.   I am a poet, I reaffirmed, ashamed

Now the music volleys through as in
a lonely moment I hear it.   Now it is all
about me.   The dance!   The verb detaches itself
seeking to become articulate   .

            And I could not help thinking
            of the wonders of the brain that
            hears that music and of our
            skill sometimes to record it.

Journey to Love

(*1955*)

For My Wife

A Negro Woman

carrying a bunch of marigolds
            wrapped
                        in an old newspaper:
She carries them upright,
            bareheaded,
                        the bulk
of her thighs
            causing her to waddle
                        as she walks
looking into
            the store window which she passes
                        on her way.
What is she
            but an ambassador
                        from another world
a world of pretty marigolds
            of two shades
                        which she announces
not knowing what she does
            other
                        than walk the streets
holding the flowers upright
            as a torch
                        so early in the morning.

The Ivy Crown

The whole process is a lie,
            unless,
                        crowned by excess,
it break forcefully,
            one way or another,
                        from its confinement—
or find a deeper well.
            Antony and Cleopatra
                        were right;
they have shown
            the way. I love you
                        or I do not live
at all.

Daffodil time
            is past. This is
                        summer, summer!
the heart says,
            and not even the full of it.
                        No doubts
are permitted—
            though they will come
                        and may
before our time
            overwhelm us.
                        We are only mortal
but being mortal
            can defy our fate.
                        We may
by an outside chance
            even win! We do not
                        look to see
jonquils and violets

come again
but there are,
still,
the roses!

Romance has no part in it.
The business of love is
cruelty *which*,
by our wills,
we transform
to live together.
It has its seasons,
for and against,
whatever the heart
fumbles in the dark
to assert
toward the end of May.
Just as the nature of briars
is to tear flesh,
I have proceeded
through them.
Keep
the briars out,
they say.
You cannot live
and keep free of
briars.

Children pick flowers.
Let them.
Though having them
in hand
they have no further use for them
but leave them crumpled
at the curb's edge.

At our age the imagination
                across the sorry facts
                                lifts us
to make roses
                stand before thorns.
                                Sure
love is cruel
                and selfish
                                and totally obtuse—
at least, blinded by the light,
                young love is.
                                But we are older,
I to love
                and you to be loved,
                                we have,
no matter how,
                by our wills survived
                                to keep
the jeweled prize
                always
                                at our finger tips.
We will it so
                and so it is
                                past all accident.

View by Color Photography
on a Commercial Calendar

The church of Vice-Morcate
                in the Canton Ticino
                                with its apple blossoms
is beautiful
                as anything I have ever seen
                                in or out of
Switzerland.
                The beauty of holiness
                                the beauty of a man's anger
reflecting his sex
                or a woman's either,
                                mountainous,
or a little stone church
                from a height
                                or
close to the camera
                the apple tree in blossom
                                or the far lake
below
                in the distance—
                                are equal
as they are unsurpassed.
                Peace
                                after the event
comes from their contemplation,
                a great peace.
                                The sky is cut off,
there is no horizon
                just the mountainside
                                bordered by water
on which tiny waves

                    without passion
                              unconcerned
cover the invisible fish.
                    And who but we are concerned
                              with the beauty of apple blossoms
and a small church
          on a promontory,
                    an ancient church—
by the look of its masonry—
          abandoned
                    by a calm lake
in the mountains
          where the sun shines
                    of a springtime
afternoon. Something
          has come to an end here,
                    it has been accomplished.

The Sparrow

(*To My Father*)

This sparrow
        who comes to sit at my window
                is a poetic truth
more than a natural one.
        His voice,
                his movements,
his habits—
        how he loves to
                flutter his wings
in the dust—
        all attest it;
                granted, he does it
to rid himself of lice
        but the relief he feels
                makes him
cry out lustily—
        which is a trait
                more related to music
than otherwise.
        Wherever he finds himself
                in early spring,
on back streets
        or beside palaces,
                he carries on
unaffectedly
        his amours.
                It begins in the egg,
his sex genders it:
        What is more pretentiously
                useless
or about which
        we more pride ourselves?

It leads as often as not
to our undoing.
                    The cockerel, the crow
                              with their challenging voices
cannot surpass
              the insistence
                        of his cheep!
Once
      at El Paso
               toward evening,
I saw—and heard!—
                ten thousand sparrows
                          who had come in from
the desert
          to roost. They filled the trees
                    of a small park. Men fled
(with ears ringing!)
                from their droppings,
                          leaving the premises
to the alligators
              who inhabit
                        the fountain. His image
is familiar
          as that of the aristocratic
                    unicorn, a pity
there are not more oats eaten
                nowadays
                        to make living easier
for him.
        At that,
              his small size,
keen eyes,
          serviceable beak
                    and general truculence
assure his survival—
                to say nothing
                        of his innumerable

130

brood.
Even the Japanese
know him
and have painted him
sympathetically,
with profound insight
into his minor
characteristics.
Nothing even remotely
subtle
about his lovemaking.
He crouches
before the female,
drags his wings,
waltzing,
throws back his head
and simply—
yells! The din
is terrific.
The way he swipes his bill
across a plank
to clean it,
is decisive.
So with everything
he does. His coppery
eyebrows
give him the air
of being always
a winner—and yet
I saw once,
the female of his species
clinging determinedly
to the edge of
a water pipe,
catch him
by his crown-feathers
to hold him

silent,
subdued,
hanging above the city streets
until
she was through with him.
What was the use
of that?
She hung there
herself,
puzzled at her success.
I laughed heartily.
Practical to the end,
it is the poem
of his existence
that triumphed
finally;
a wisp of feathers
flattened to the pavement,
wings spread symmetrically
as if in flight,
the head gone,
the black escutcheon of the breast
undecipherable,
an effigy of a sparrow,
a dried wafer only,
left to say
and it says it
without offense,
beautifully;
This was I,
a sparrow.
I did my best;
farewell.

The King!

Nell Gwyn,
         it says in the dictionary,
                  actress
and mistress of Charles the Second:
         what a lot
                  of pious rot there is
surrounding
         that
                  simple statement.
She waked in the morning,
         bathed in
                  the King's bountiful
water
         which enveloped her
                  completely and,
magically,
         with the grit, took away
                  all her sins.
It was the King's body
         which was served;
                  the King's boards which
in the evening
         she capably trod;
                  she fed
the King's poor
         and when she died,
                  left them some slight moneys
under certain
         conditions.

Happy the woman
         whose husband makes her
                  the "King's whore."
All this you will find

in the dictionary
                    where it has been
preserved forever—
            since it is beautiful
                    and true.

The Lady Speaks

A storm raged among the live oaks
                while my husband and I
                        sat in the semi-dark
listening!
            We watched from the windows,
                    the lights off,
saw the moss
            whipped upright
                    by the wind's force.
Two candles we had lit
            side by side
                    before us
so solidly had our house been built
            kept their tall flames
                    unmoved.
May it be so
            when a storm sends the moss
                    whipping
back and forth
            upright
                    above my head
like flames in the final
            fury.

Tribute to the Painters

Satyrs dance!
            all the deformities take wing
                        centaurs
leading to the rout of the vocables
            in the writings
of Gertrude
            Stein—but
                        you cannot be
an artist
            by mere ineptitude
The dream
            is in pursuit!

The neat figures of
            Paul Klee
                        fill the canvas
but that
            is not the work
                        of a child
The cure began, perhaps,
            with the abstractions
                        of Arabic art
Dürer
            with his *Melancholy*
                        was ware of it—
the shattered masonry. Leonardo
            saw it,
                        the obsession,
and ridiculed it
            in *La Gioconda*.
                        Bosch's
congeries of tortured souls and devils
            who prey on them
                        fish

swallowing
>their own entrails

Freud
>Picasso
>>Juan Gris.

The letter from a friend
>saying:
>>For the last

three nights
>I have slept like a baby
>>without

liquor or dope of any sort!
>We know
>>that a stasis

from a chrysalis
>has stretched its wings—
>>like a bull

or the Minotaur
>or Beethoven
>>in the scherzo

of his 9th Symphony
>stomped
>>his heavy feet

I saw love
>mounted naked on a horse
>>on a swan

the back of a fish
>the bloodthirsty conger eel
>>and laughed

recalling the Jew
>in the pit
>>among his fellows

when the indifferent chap
>with the machine gun
>>was spraying the heap.

He
       had not yet been hit
              but smiled
comforting his companions.

Dreams possess me
       and the dance
              of my thoughts
involving animals
       the blameless beasts
and there came to me
       just now
              the knowledge of
the tyranny of the image
       and how
              men
in their designs
       have learned
              to shatter it
whatever it may be,
       that the trouble
              in their minds
shall be quieted,
       put to bed
              again.

To a Man Dying on His Feet

—not that we are not all
        "dying on our feet"
                but the look you give me
and to which I bow,
        is more immediate.
                It is keenly alert,
suspicious of me—
        as of all that are living—and
                apologetic.
Your jaw
        wears the stubble
                of a haggard beard,
a dirty beard,
        which resembles
                the snow through which
your long legs
        are conducting you.
                Whither? Where are you going?
This would be a fine day
        to go on a journey.
                Say to Florida
where at this season
        all go
                nowadays.
There grows the hibiscus,
        the star jasmine
                and more than I can tell
but the odors
        from what I know
                must be alluring.
Come with me there!
        you look like a good guy,
                come this evening.

The plane leaves at 6:30
                or have you another
                                appointment?

Come on!

A different kind of thought
                blander
                                and more desperate
like that of
                Sergeant So-and-So
                                at the road
in Belleau Wood:
                Come on!
                                Do you want to live
forever?—
                That
                                is the essence
of poetry.
                But it does not
                                always
take the same form.
                For the most part
                                it consists
in listening
                to the nightingale
                                or fools.

The Pink Locust

I'm persistent as the pink locust,
                once admitted
                                to the garden,
you will not easily get rid of it.
                Tear it from the ground,
                                if one hair-thin rootlet
remain
                it will come again.
                        It is
flattering to think of myself
                so. It is also
                                laughable.
A modest flower,
                resembling a pink sweet-pea,
                                you cannot help
but admire it
                until its habits
                        become known.
Are we not most of us
                like that? It would be
                      too much
if the public
                pried among the minutiae
                        of our private affairs.
Not
                that we have anything to hide
                      but could *they*
stand it? Of course
                the world would be gratified
                      to find out
what fools we have made of ourselves.
                The question is,
                      would they

be generous with us—
        as we have been
                with others? It is,
as I say,
        a flower
                incredibly resilient
under attack!
        Neglect it
                and it will grow into a tree.
I wish I could *so* think of myself
        and of what
                is to become of me.
The poet himself,
        what does he think of himself
                facing his world?
It will not do to say,
        as he is inclined to say:
                Not much. The poem
would be in *that* betrayed.
        He might as well answer—
                "a rose is a rose
is a rose" and let it go at that.
        A rose *is* a rose
                and the poem equals it
if it be well made.
        The poet
                cannot slight himself
without slighting
        his poem—
                which would be
ridiculous.
        Life offers
                no greater reward.
And so,
        like this flower,
                I persist—

for what there may be in it.
        I am not,
                I know,
in the galaxy of poets
        a rose
                but *who*, among the rest,
will deny me
        my place.

Classic Picture

It is a classic picture,
        women have always fussed with their hair
                (having no sisters
I never watched the process
        so intimately
                as this time); the reason for it
is not clear—
        tho' I acknowledge,
                an unkempt head of hair,
while not as repulsive as a nest of snakes,
        is repulsive enough
                in a woman.
Therefore
        she fusses with her hair
                for
a woman does not want to seem repulsive,
        unless
                to gain for herself

she be hungry,
            hungry!
                        as would be a man
and all hunger is repulsive
            and puts on
                        an ugly face.
Their heads are not made as a man's,
            an ornament
                        in itself. They have
other charms—
            needless
                        to enumerate. Under
their ornate coiffures
            lurks a specter,
                        coiling snakes
doubling for tresses

A woman's brains
            which can be keen
                        are condemned,
like a poet's,
            to what deceptions she can muster
                        to lead men
to their ruin.
            But look more deeply
                        into her maneuvers,
and puzzle as we will about them
            they may mean
                        anything

Address:

To a look in my son's eyes—
   I hope he did not see
      that I was looking—
that I have seen
   often enough
      in the mirror,
a male look
   approaching despair—
      there is a female look
to match it
   no need to speak of that:
      Perhaps
it was only a dreamy look
   not an unhappy one
      but absent
from the world—
   such as plagued the eyes
      of Bobby Burns
in his youth and threw him
   into the arms
      of women—
in which he could
   forget himself,
      not defiantly,
but with full acceptance
   of his lot
      as a man
His Jean forgave him
   and took him to her heart
      time after time
when he would be
   too drunk
      with Scotch

or the love of other women
                    to notice
                              what he was doing.
What was he intent upon
                    but to drown out
                              that look? What
does it portend?
                    A war
                              will not erase it
nor a bank account,
                    estlin,
                              amounting to 9 figures.
Flow gently sweet Afton
                    among thy green braes—
                              no matter
that he wrote the song
                    to another woman
                              it was never for sale.

The Drunk and the Sailor

The petty fury
        that disrupts my life—
                at the striking of a wrong key
as if it had been
        a woman lost
or a fortune   . .
        The man was obviously drunk,
                Christopher Marlowe
could have been no drunker
        when he got himself
                stuck through the eye
with a poniard.
        The bus station was crowded.
The man
        heavy-set
                about my own age
seventy
        was talking privately
            with a sailor.
He had an ugly jaw on him.
        Suddenly
                sitting there on the bench
too drunk to stand
        he began menacingly
            his screaming.
The young sailor
        who could have flattened him
            at one blow
kept merely looking at him.
        The nerve-tingling screeches
            that sprang
sforzando
        from that stubble beard

                    would have distinguished
an operatic tenor.
          But me—
                    the shock of it—
my heart leaped in my chest
          so that I saw red
                    wanted
to strangle the guy
          The fury of love
                    is no less.

A Smiling Dane

The Danish native
            before the Christian era
                        whose body
features intact
            with a rope
                        also intact
round the neck
            found recently
                        in a peat bog
is dead.
                        Are you surprised?
                        You should be.
The diggers
            who discovered him
                        expected more.
Frightened
            they quit the place
                        thinking
his ghost might walk.

The cast of his features
            shows him
                        to be
a man of intelligence.
            It did him no good.
                        What his eyes saw
cannot be more
            than the male
                        and female
of it—
            if as much.
                        His stomach
its contents examined
            shows him
                        before he died

to have had
      a meal
                consisting of local grains
swallowed whole
      which he probably enjoyed
            though he did not
much as we do
      chew them.
            And what if
the image of his frightened executioners
      is not recorded?
            Do we not know
their features
      as if
            it had occurred
today?
      We can still see in his smile
            their grimaces.

Shadows

Shadows cast by the street light
        under the stars,
                the head is tilted back,
the long shadow of the legs
        presumes a world
                taken for granted
on which the cricket trills.
        The hollows of the eyes
                are unpeopled.
Right and left
        climb the ladders of night
                as dawn races
to put out the stars.
        That
                is the poetic figure
but we know
        better: what is not now
                will never
be. Sleep secure,
        the little dog in the snapshot
                keeps his shrewd eyes
pared. Memory
        is liver than sight.
                A man
looking out,
        seeing the shadows—
                it is himself
that can be painlessly amputated
        by a mere shifting
                of the stars.
A comfort so easily not to be

and to be at once one
                    with every man.
The night blossoms
                    with a thousand shadows
                              so long
as there are stars,
                    street lights
                              or a moon and
who shall say
                    by their shadows
which is different
                    from the other
                              fat or lean.

                              II

Ripped from the concept of our lives
                    and from all concept
                              somehow, and plainly,
the sun will come up
                    each morning
                              and sink again.
So that we experience
                    violently
                              every day
two worlds
                    one of which we share with the
                    rose in bloom
                              and one,
by far the greater,
                    with the past,
                              the world of memory,
the silly world of history,
                    the world
                              of the imagination.

Which leaves only the beasts and trees,
    crystals
            with their refractive
            surfaces
and rotting things
    to stir our wonder.
            Save for the little
central hole
    of the eye itself
        into which
we dare not stare too hard
    or we are lost.
        The instant
trivial as it is
    is all we have
        unless—unless
things the imagination feeds upon,
    the scent of the rose,
        startle us anew.

Asphodel, That Greeny Flower

BOOK I

Of asphodel, that greeny flower,
        like a buttercup
                upon its branching stem—
save that it's green and wooden—
        I come, my sweet,
                to sing to you.
We lived long together
        a life filled,
                if you will,
with flowers. So that
        I was cheered
                when I came first to know
that there were flowers also
        in hell.
                Today
I'm filled with the fading memory of those flowers
        that we both loved,
                even to this poor
colorless thing—
        I saw it
                when I was a child—
little prized among the living
        but the dead see,
                asking among themselves:
What do I remember
        that was shaped
                as this thing is shaped?
while our eyes fill
        with tears.
                Of love, abiding love
it will be telling

though too weak a wash of crimson
colors it
to make it wholly credible.
There is something
something urgent
I have to say to you
and you alone
but it must wait
while I drink in
the joy of your approach,
perhaps for the last time.
And so
with fear in my heart
I drag it out
and keep on talking
for I dare not stop.
Listen while I talk on
against time.
It will not be
for long.
I have forgot
and yet I see clearly enough
something
central to the sky
which ranges round it.
An odor
springs from it!
A sweetest odor!
Honeysuckle! And now
there comes the buzzing of a bee!
and a whole flood
of sister memories!
Only give me time,
time to recall them
before I shall speak out.
Give me time,
time.

154

When I was a boy
            I kept a book
                        to which, from time
to time,
            I added pressed flowers
                        until, after a time,
I had a good collection.
            The asphodel,
                        forebodingly,
among them.
            I bring you,
                        reawakened,
a memory of those flowers.
            They were sweet
                        when I pressed them
and retained
            something of their sweetness
                        a long time.
It is a curious odor,
            a moral odor,
                        that brings me
near to you.
            The color
                        was the first to go.
There had come to me
            a challenge,
                        your dear self,
mortal as I was,
      :   the lily's throat
                        to the hummingbird!
Endless wealth,
            I thought,
                        held out its arms to me.
A thousand topics
            in an apple blossom.
                        The generous earth itself

155

gave us lief.
                    The whole world
                              became my garden!
But the sea
          which no one tends
                    is also a garden
when the sun strikes it
          and the waves
                    are wakened.
I have seen it
          and so have you
                    when it puts all flowers
to shame.
                    Too, there are the starfish
                              stiffened by the sun
and other sea wrack
          and weeds. We knew that
                    along with the rest of it
for we were born by the sea,
          knew its rose hedges
                    to the very water's brink.
There the pink mallow grows
          and in their season
                    strawberries
and there, later,
          we went to gather
                    the wild plum.
I cannot say
          that I have gone to hell
                    for your love
but often
          found myself there
                    in your pursuit.
I do not like it
          and wanted to be
                    in heaven. Hear me out.

Do not turn away.

I have learned much in my life
          from books
                    and out of them
about love.
          Death
                    is not the end of it.
There is a hierarchy
          which can be attained,
                    I think,
in its service.
          Its guerdon
                    is a fairy flower;
a cat of twenty lives.
          If no one came to try it
                    the world
would be the loser.
          It has been
                    for you and me
as one who watches a storm
          come in over the water.
                    We have stood
from year to year
          before the spectacle of our lives
                    with joined hands.
The storm unfolds.
          Lightning
                    plays about the edges of the clouds.
The sky to the north
          is placid,
                    blue in the afterglow
as the storm piles up.
          It is a flower
                    that will soon reach
the apex of its bloom.
          We danced,

in our minds,
and read a book together.
                    You remember?
                        It was a serious book.
And so books
            entered our lives.
The sea! The sea!
            Always
                        when I think of the sea
there comes to mind
            the *Iliad*
                        and Helen's public fault
that bred it.
            Were it not for that
                        there would have been
no poem but the world
            if we had remembered,
                        those crimson petals
spilled among the stones,
            would have called it simply
                        murder.
The sexual orchid that bloomed then
            sending so many
                        disinterested
men to their graves
            has left its memory
                        to a race of fools
or heroes
            if silence is a virtue.
                        The sea alone
with its multiplicity
            holds any hope.
                        The storm
has proven abortive
            but we remain
                        after the thoughts it roused

to
        re-cement our lives.
           It is the mind
the mind
        that must be cured
           short of death's
intervention,
        and the will becomes again
           a garden. The poem
is complex and the place made
        in our lives
           for the poem.
Silence can be complex too,
        but you do not get far
           with silence.
Begin again.
        It is like Homer's
           catalogue of ships:
it fills up the time.
        I speak in figures,
           well enough, the dresses
you wear are figures also,
        we could not meet
           otherwise. When I speak
of flowers
        it is to recall
           that at one time
we were young.
        All women are not Helen,
           I know that,
but have Helen in their hearts.
        My sweet,
           you have it also, therefore
I love you
        and could not love you otherwise.
           Imagine you saw

a field made up of women
                all silver-white.
                        What should you do
but love them?
                The storm bursts
                        or fades! it is not
the end of the world.
                Love is something else,
                        or so I thought it,
a garden which expands,
                though I knew you as a woman
                        and never thought otherwise,
until the whole sea
                has been taken up
                        and all its gardens.
It was the love of love,
                the love that swallows up all else,
                        a grateful love,
a love of nature, of people,
                animals,
                        a love engendering
gentleness and goodness
                that moved me
                        and *that* I saw in you.
I should have known
                though I did not,
                        that the lily-of-the-valley
is a flower makes many ill
                who whiff it.
                        We had our children,
rivals in the general onslaught.
                I put them aside
                        though I cared for them
as well as any man
                could care for his children
                        according to my lights.

You understand
             I had to meet you
                      after the event
and have still to meet you.
             Love
                      to which you too shall bow
along with me—
             a flower
                      a weakest flower
shall be our trust
             and not because
                      we are too feeble
to do otherwise
             but because
                      at the height of my power
I risked what I had to do,
             therefore to prove
                      that we love each other
while my very bones sweated
             that I could not cry to you
                      in the act.
Of asphodel, that greeny flower,
             I come, my sweet,
                      to sing to you!
My heart rouses
             thinking to bring you news
                      of something
that concerns you
             and concerns many men. Look at
                      what passes for the new.
You will not find it there but in
             despised poems.
                      It is difficult
to get the news from poems
             yet men die miserably every day
                      for lack

of what is found there.
Hear me out
for I too am concerned
and every man
who wants to die at peace in his bed
besides.

BOOK II

Approaching death,
as we think, the death of love,
no distinction
any more suffices to differentiate
the particulars
of place and condition
with which we have been long
familiar.
All appears
as if seen
wavering through water.
We start awake with a cry
of recognition
but soon the outlines
become again vague.
If we are to understand our time,
we must find the key to it,
not in the eighteenth
and nineteenth centuries,
but in earlier, wilder
and darker epochs . .
So to know, what I have to know
about my own death,
if it be real,

I have to take it apart.
                  What does your generation think
                        of Cézanne?
I asked a young artist.
                  The abstractions of Hindu painting,
                        he replied,
is all at the moment which interests me.
                  He liked my poem
                        about the parts
of a broken bottle,
                  lying green in the cinders
                        of a hospital courtyard.
There was also, to his mind,
                  the one on gay wallpaper
                        which he had heard about
but not read.
                  I was grateful to him
                        for his interest.
Do you remember
                  how at Interlaken
                        we were waiting, four days,
to see the Jungfrau
                  but rain had fallen steadily.
                        Then
just before train time
                  on a tip from one of the waitresses
                        we rushed
to the Gipfel Platz
                  and there it was!
                        in the distance
covered with new-fallen snow.
                  When I was at Granada,
                        I remember,
in the overpowering heat
                  climbing a treeless hill
                        overlooking the Alhambra.

At my appearance at the summit
        two small boys
            who had been playing
there
        made themselves scarce.
            Starting to come down
by a new path
        I at once found myself surrounded
            by gypsy women
who came up to me,
        I could speak little Spanish,
            and directed me,
guided by a young girl,
        on my way.
            These were the pinnacles.
The deaths I suffered
        began in the heads
            about me, my eyes
were too keen
        not to see through
            the world's niggardliness.
I accepted it
        as my fate.
            The wealthy
I defied
        or not so much they,
            for they have their uses,
as they who take their cues from them.
        I lived
            to breathe above the stench
not knowing how I in my own person
        would be overcome
            finally. I was lost
failing the poem.
        But if I have come from the sea
            it is not to be

wholly
                fascinated by the glint of waves.
                                The free interchange
of light over their surface
                which I have compared
                                to a garden
should not deceive us
                or prove
                                too difficult a figure.
The poem
                if it reflects the sea
                                reflects only
its dance
                upon that profound depth
                                where
it seems to triumph.
                The bomb puts an end
                                to all that.
I am reminded
                that the bomb
                                also
is a flower
                dedicated
                                howbeit
to our destruction.
                The mere picture
                                of the exploding bomb
fascinates us
                so that we cannot wait
                                to prostrate ourselves
before it. We do not believe
                that love
                                can so wreck our lives.
The end
                will come
                                in its time.

Meanwhile
        we are sick to death
                of the bomb
and its childlike
        insistence.
                Death is no answer,
no answer—
        to a blind old man
                whose bones
have the movement
        of the sea,
                a sexless old man
for whom it is a sea
        of which his verses
                are made up.
There is no power
        so great as love
                which is a sea,
which is a garden—
        as enduring
                as the verses
of that blind old man
        destined
                to live forever.
Few men believe that
        nor in the games of children.
                They believe rather
in the bomb
        and shall die by
                the bomb.
Compare Darwin's voyage of the *Beagle*,
        a voyage of discovery if there ever was one,
                to the death
incommunicado
        in the electric chair
                of the Rosenbergs.

It is the mark of the times
            that though we condemn
                        what they stood for
we admire their fortitude.
            But Darwin
                        opened our eyes
to the gardens of the world,
            as *they* closed them.
                        Or take that other voyage
which promised so much
            but due to the world's avarice
                        breeding hatred
through fear,
            ended so disastrously;
                        a voyage
with which I myself am so deeply concerned,
            that of the *Pinta*,
                        the *Niña*
and the *Santa María*.
            How the world opened its eyes!
                        It was a flower
upon which April
            had descended from the skies!
                        How bitter
a disappointment!
            In all,
                        this led mainly
to the deaths I have suffered.
            For there had been kindled
                        more minds
than that of the discoverers
            and set dancing
                        to a measure,
a new measure!
            Soon lost.
                        The measure itself

has been lost
            and we suffer for it.
                        We come to our deaths
in silence.
            The bomb speaks.
                        All suppressions,
from the witchcraft trials at Salem
            to the latest
                        book burnings
are confessions
            that the bomb
                        has entered our lives
to destroy us.
            Every drill
                        driven into the earth
for oil enters my side
            also.
                        Waste, waste!
dominates the world.
            It is the bomb's work.
                        What else was the fire
at the Jockey Club in Buenos Aires
            (*malos aires*, we should say)
                        when with Perón's connivance
the hoodlums destroyed,
            along with the books
                        the priceless Goyas
that hung there?
            You know how we treasured
                        the few paintings
we still cling to
            especially the one
                        by the dead
Charlie Demuth.
            With your smiles
                        and other trivia of the sort

my secret life
　　　　has been made up,
　　　　　　　some baby's life
which had been lost
　　　　had I not intervened.
　　　　　　　But the words
made solely of air
　　　　or less,
　　　　　　　that came to me
out of the air
　　　　and insisted
　　　　　　　on being written down,
I regret most—
　　　　that there has come an end
　　　　　　　to them.
For in spite of it all,
　　　　all that I have brought on myself,
　　　　　　　grew that single image
that I adore
　　　　equally with you
　　　　　　　and so
it brought us together.

BOOK III

What power has love but forgiveness?
　　　　In other words
　　　　　　　by its intervention
what has been done
　　　　can be undone.
　　　　　　　What good is it otherwise?
Because of this
　　　　I have invoked the flower
　　　　　　　in that

frail as it is
                    after winter's harshness
                            it comes again
to delect us.
                    Asphodel, the ancients believed,
                            in hell's despite
was such a flower.
                    With daisies pied
                            and violets blue,
we say, the spring of the year
                    comes in!
                            So may it be
with the spring of love's year
                    also
                            if we can but find
the secret word
                    to transform it.
                            It is ridiculous
what airs we put on
                    to seem profound
                            while our hearts
gasp dying
                    for want of love.
                            Having your love
I was rich.
                    Thinking to have lost it
                            I am tortured
and cannot rest.
                    I do not come to you
                            abjectly
with confessions of my faults,
                    I have confessed,
                            all of them.
In the name of love
                    I come proudly
                            as to an equal

to be forgiven.
            Let me, for I know
                        you take it hard,
with good reason,
            give the steps
                        if it may be
by which you shall mount,
            again to think well
                        of me.
The statue
            of Colleoni's horse
                        with the thickset little man
on top
            in armor
                        presenting a naked sword
comes persistently
            to my mind.
                        And with him
the horse rampant
            roused by the mare in
                        the Venus and Adonis.
These are pictures
            of crude force.
                        Once at night
waiting at a station
            with a friend
                        a fast freight
thundered through
            kicking up the dust.
                        My friend,
a distinguished artist,
            turned with me
                        to protect his eyes:
That's what we'd all like to be, Bill,
            he said. I smiled
                        knowing how deeply

he meant it. I saw another man
                yesterday
                        in the subway.
I was on my way uptown
        to a meeting.
                        He kept looking at me
and I at him:
                He had a worn knobbed stick
                        between his knees
suitable
        to keep off dogs,
                        a man of perhaps forty.
He wore a beard
        parted in the middle,
                a black beard,
and a hat,
        a brown felt hat
                        lighter than
his skin. His eyes,
        which were intelligent,
                were wide open
but evasive, mild.
                I was frankly curious
                        and looked at him
closely. He was slight of build
                but robust enough
                        had on
a double-breasted black coat
                and a vest
                        which showed at the neck
the edge of a heavy and very dirty
                undershirt.
                        His trousers
were striped
                and a lively
                        reddish brown. His shoes

which were good
                if somewhat worn
                                had been recently polished.
His brown socks
                were about his ankles.
                                In his breast pocket
he carried
                a gold fountain pen
                                and a mechanical
pencil. For some reason
                which I could not fathom
                                I was unable
to keep my eyes off him.
                A worn leather zipper case
                                bulging with its contents
lay between his ankles
                on the floor.
                                Then I remembered:
When my father was a young man—
                it came to me
                                from an old photograph—
he wore such a beard.
                This man
                                reminds me of my father.
I am looking
                into my father's
                                face! Some surface
of some advertising sign
                is acting
                                as a reflector. It is
my own.
                But at once
                                the car grinds to a halt.
Speak to him,
                I cried. He
                                will know the secret.

He was gone
        and I did nothing about it.
                With him
went all men
        and all women too
                were in his loins.
Fanciful or not
        it seemed to me
                a flower
whose savor had been lost.
        It was a flower
                some exotic orchid
that Herman Melville had admired
        in the
                Hawaiian jungle.
Or the lilacs
        of men who left their marks,
                by torchlight,
rituals of the hunt,
        on the walls
                of prehistoric
caves in the Pyrenees—
        what draftsmen they were—
                bison and deer.
Their women
        had big buttocks.
                But what
draftsmen they were!
        By my father's beard,
                what draftsmen.
And so, by chance,
        how should it be otherwise?
                from what came to me
in a subway train
        I build a picture
                of all men.

It is winter
          and there
                    waiting for you to care for them
are your plants.
          Poor things! you say
              as you compassionately
pour at their roots
          the reviving water.
              Lean-cheeked
I say to myself
          kindness moves her
              shall she not be kind
also to me? At this
          courage possessed me finally
              to go on.
Sweet, creep into my arms!
          I spoke hurriedly
              in the spell
of some wry impulse
          when I boasted
              that there was
any pride left in me.
          Do not believe it.
              Unless
in a special way,
          a way I shrink to speak of
              I am proud. After that manner
I call on you
          as I do on myself the same
              to forgive all women
who have offended you.
          It is the artist's failing
              to seek and to yield
such forgiveness.
          It will cure us both.
              Let us

keep it to ourselves but trust it.
                  These heads
                          that stick up all around me
are, I take it,
              also proud.
                          But the flowers
know at least this much,
                  that it is not spring
                          and will be proud only
in the proper season.
                  A trance holds men.
                          They are dazed
and their faces in the public print
                  show it. We follow them
                          as children followed
the Pied Piper
              of Hamelin—but he
                          was primarily
interested only in rats.
                  I say to you
                          privately
that the heads of most men I see
                  at meetings
                          or when I come up against them
elsewhere
          are full of cupidity.
                          Let us breed
from those others.
                  They are the flowers of the race.
                          The asphodel
poor as it is
              is among them.
                          But in their pride
there come to my mind
                  the daisy,
                          not the shy flower

of England but the brilliance
            that mantled
                        with white
the fields
            which we knew
                        as children.
Do you remember
            their spicy-sweet
                        odor? What abundance!
There are many other flowers·
            I could recall
                        for your pleasure:
the small yellow sweet-scented violet
            that grew
                        in marshy places!
You were like those
            though I quickly
                        correct myself
for you were a woman
            and no flower
                        and had to face
the problems which confront a woman.
            But you were for all that
                        flowerlike
and I say this to you now
            and it is the thing
                        which compounded
my torment
            that I never
                        forgot it.
You have forgiven me
            making me new again.
                        So that here
in the place
            dedicated in the imagination
                        to memory

of the dead
          I bring you
                    a last flower. Don't think
that because I say this
          in a poem
                    it can be treated lightly
or that the facts will not uphold it.
          Are facts not flowers
                    and flowers facts
or poems flowers
          or all works of the imagination,
                    interchangeable?
Which proves
          that love
                    rules them all, for then
you will be my queen,
          my queen of love
                    forever more.

CODA

Inseparable from the fire
          its light
                    takes precedence over it.
Then follows
          what we have dreaded—
                    but it can never
overcome what has gone before.
          In the huge gap
                    between the flash
and the thunderstroke
          spring has come in
                    or a deep snow fallen.
Call it old age.
          In that stretch
                    we have lived to see

a colt kick up his heels.
            Do not hasten
                        laugh and play
in an eternity
            the heat will not overtake the light.
                        That's sure.
That gelds the bomb,
            permitting
                        that the mind contain it.
This is that interval,
            that sweetest interval,
                        when love will blossom,
come early, come late
            and give itself to the lover.
Only the imagination is real!
            I have declared it
                        time without end.
If a man die
            it is because death
                has first
possessed his imagination.
            But if he refuse death—
                        no greater evil
can befall him
            unless it be the death of love
                        meet him
in full career.
            Then indeed
                for him
the light has gone out.
But love and the imagination
            are of a piece,
                        swift as the light
to avoid destruction.
            So we come to watch time's flight
                as we might watch

summer lightning
   or fireflies, secure,
      by grace of the imagination,
safe in its care.
    For if
      the light itself
has escaped,
    the whole edifice opposed to it
      goes down.
Light, the imagination
    and love,
      in our age,
by natural law,
    which we worship,
      maintain
all of a piece
    their dominance.
So let us love
    confident as is the light
      in its struggle with darkness
that there is as much to say
    and more
      for the one side
and that not the darker
    which John Donne
      for instance
among many men
    presents to us.
      In the controversy
touching the younger
    and the older Tolstoi,
      Villon, St. Anthony, Kung,
Rimbaud, Buddha
    and Abraham Lincoln
      the palm goes
always to the light;

Who most shall advance the light—
　　　　call it what you may!
The light
　　　　for all time shall outspeed
　　　　　　the thunder crack.
Medieval pageantry
　　　　is human and we enjoy
　　　　　　the rumor of it
as in our world we enjoy
　　　　the reading of Chaucer,
　　　　　　likewise
a priest's raiment
　　　　(or that of a savage chieftain).
　　　　　　It is all
a celebration of the light.
　　　　　　All the pomp and ceremony
　　　　　　　　of weddings,
"Sweet Thames, run softly
　　　　till I end
　　　　　　my song,"—
are of an equal sort.
For our wedding, too,
　　　　the light was wakened
　　　　　　and shone. The light!
the light stood before us
　　　　waiting!
　　　　　　I thought the world
stood still.
　　　　At the altar
　　　　　　so intent was I
before my vows,
　　　　so moved by your presence
　　　　　　a girl so pale
and ready to faint
　　　　that I pitied
　　　　　　and wanted to protect you.

As I think of it now,
           after a lifetime,
                     it is as if
a sweet-scented flower
           were poised
                     and for me did open.
Asphodel
           has no odor
                     save to the imagination
but it too
           celebrates the light.
                     It is late
but an odor
           as from our wedding
                     has revived for me
and begun again to penetrate
           into all crevices
                     of my world.

Ten Years of a New Rhythm

These poems were written over a period of less than ten years: the earliest, perhaps, is "To the Ghost of Marjorie Kinnan Rawlings," who died in 1953; "Heel and Toe" was written in 1961. Most of them utilize the triadic stanza and the "measured line," a discovery Dr. Williams made in *Paterson II*, beginning with "The descent beckons / as the ascent beckons," exhibited here in regular form in *Pictures from Brueghel*. I say "regular form," but, of course, Dr. Williams has adhered to no regular form since his *Poems: 1909*. With the Imagists, he practiced free verse; but in 1924 he rejected free verse ("This Florida") and sought for a controlled measure. This measure he was not to find until *Paterson*, developing the "variable foot" which produced *versos sueltos*, "loose verses," as he called them.

There was the danger that even with the "variable foot," the triadic stanza might become monotonous as free verse had become monotonous. It was "measure" that rescued Williams' verse by rhythmical variations, as the blank verse of Shakespeare and Milton was rescued by rhythmical variations of iambic pentameter. "The iamb is not the normal measure of American speech," he told me in 1953. "The foot has to be expanded or contracted in terms of actual speech. The key to modern poetry is *measure*, which must reflect the flux of modern life. You should find a variable measure for the fixed measure; for man and the poet must keep pace with this world."

Adhering quite rigorously to the triad in *Desert Music* and *Journey to Love*, Williams found that this form, even when measured, could not completely express the modern idiom. "The Gossips," one of the latest of these poems, runs to the sonnet length of fourteen lines (in form, of course, it is anything but a sonnet); "The Stone Crock" and "Poem—On Getting a Card . . . from a Poet I Love" (E. E. Cummings) use the triadic pattern with a short fourth line to fill out the measure; "The Dance" and "Portrait of a Woman at Her Bath" run in almost regular quatrain form; "Some Simple Measures in the American Idiom and the Variable Foot" vary from verse form to verse form, controlled always, however, by the measure of the "variable foot." "Tapiola" (1959), looks and sounds suspiciously like free verse.

"How shall we get said what must be said?" Williams asks in *The Desert Music*: "Only the poem. / Only the counted poem, to an exact measure:" is his answer.

As he refined his measured line, Williams' poetry continued to improve. Many critics find some of his best poems written in the last ten years. Indeed, this crowning measure of his poetic line led Kenneth Rexroth to call him "the first American classic": ". . . his poetic line is organically welded to American speech like muscle to bone, as the choruses of Euripides were welded to the speech of the Athenians in the market place."

JOHN C. THIRLWALL
The City College of New York

Index of Poems by Titles